IN THE AIR!

Written by Claire Philip

Illustrated by Maxine Lee-Mackie

T0004640

WINDMILL BOOKS

Published in 2023 by Windmill Books,
an Imprint of Rosen Publishing
2544 Clinton St.
Buffalo, NY 14224

Copyright © 2021 by Miles Kelly Publishing

Cataloging-in-Publication Data

Names: Philip, Claire, author. | Lee-Mackie, Maxine, illustrator.
Title: In the air! / by Claire Philip, illustrated by Maxine Lee-Mackie.
Description: New York : Windmill Books, 2023. | Series: On the go!
Identifiers: ISBN 9781538392706 (pbk.) | ISBN 9781538392713 (library bound) | ISBN 9781538392720 (ebook)
Subjects: LCSH: Flying-machines--Pictorial works--Juvenile literature. | Airplanes--Pictorial works--Juvenile literature.
Classification: LCC TL547P455 2023 | DDC 629.133--d

Printed in the United States of America

CPSIA Compliance Information: Batch #CWWM23
For Further Information contact Rosen Publishing at 1-800-237-9932

Find us on

Let's fly!

Every day, planes of different sizes carry people and cargo around the world.

Boeing 747

Cargo plane

Cargo planes have huge storage areas that take up most of the plane!

I can carry tons of cargo!

Airbus A320

Super-sized

This Airbus A380 is currently the biggest airplane in the world!

Airflow

Lift

Wing

With two levels of seating for its passengers, the Airbus A380 is like a massive double-decker bus.

Planes can fly because of an invisible force known as "lift." As the plane flies, air moves over its wings. The quicker the air travels over the wings, the more lift is created.

I can carry more than 850 passengers!

This mighty plane can fly very long distances without needing to stop for fuel – around 17 hours!

Propeller power!

Propellers help aircraft move forward by creating a force called thrust. They are powered by a plane's engine.

Flying upside down is my favorite trick!

Propeller

Monoplane

Most planes today are monoplanes, meaning they only have one set of wings.

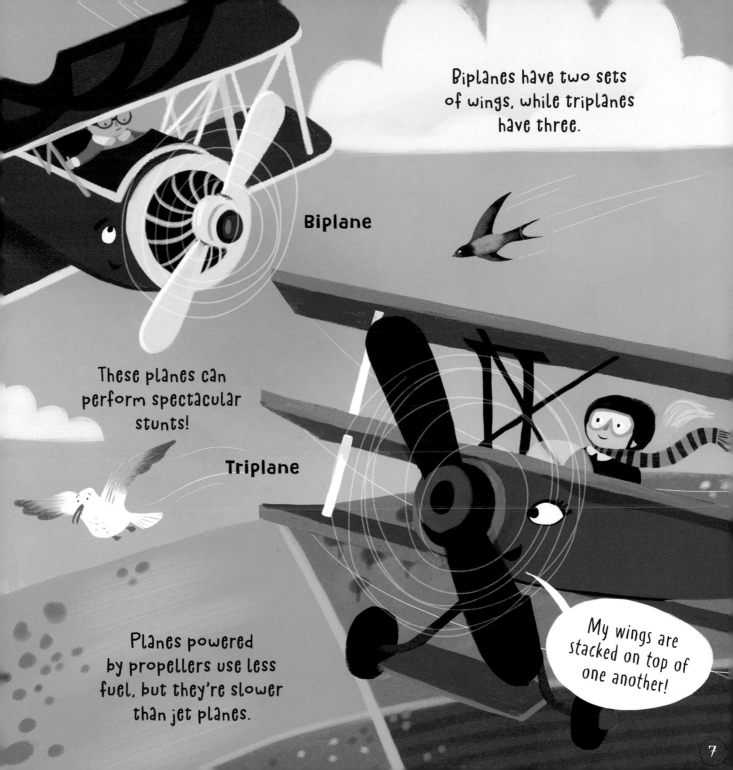

Biplanes have two sets of wings, while triplanes have three.

Biplane

These planes can perform spectacular stunts!

Triplane

Planes powered by propellers use less fuel, but they're slower than jet planes.

My wings are stacked on top of one another!

Landing on water

Splash! Did you know that some planes can land on, and take off from, water?

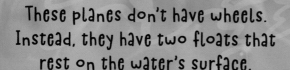

Time to go!

Floatplanes are used to get to remote islands that don't have space for long runways.

These planes don't have wheels. Instead, they have two floats that rest on the water's surface.

If the weather is stormy, floatplanes can't fly – it would be too dangerous to try to land on choppy waters.

Welcome aboard!

The main body of the plane, called the fuselage, doesn't touch the water.

9

In an emergency

Many emergency services are air-based, as they can get to locations very quickly.

In some places, wildfires are common. Special fire-fighting tanker planes fly over the flames and drop huge amounts of water.

We're going to need more water!

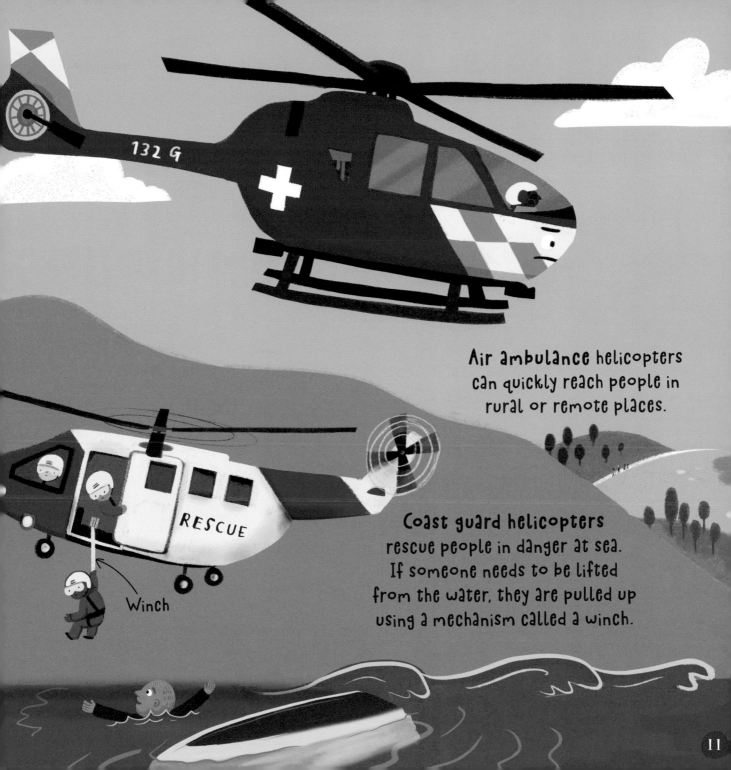

132 G

Air ambulance helicopters can quickly reach people in rural or remote places.

RESCUE

Winch

Coast guard helicopters rescue people in danger at sea. If someone needs to be lifted from the water, they are pulled up using a mechanism called a winch.

High fliers

There are lots of ways to take to the sky.
How many of these have you seen?

Wing suit

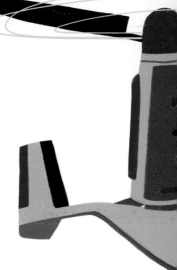

Light sport
aircraft

Microlight

Autogyro

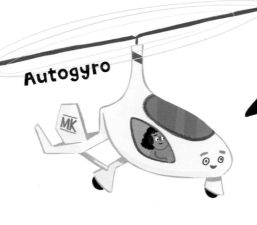

A jet pack can
help me fly short
distances!

Gyrodyne

Jet pack

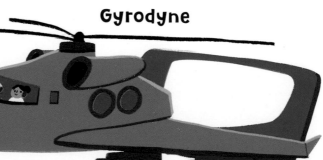

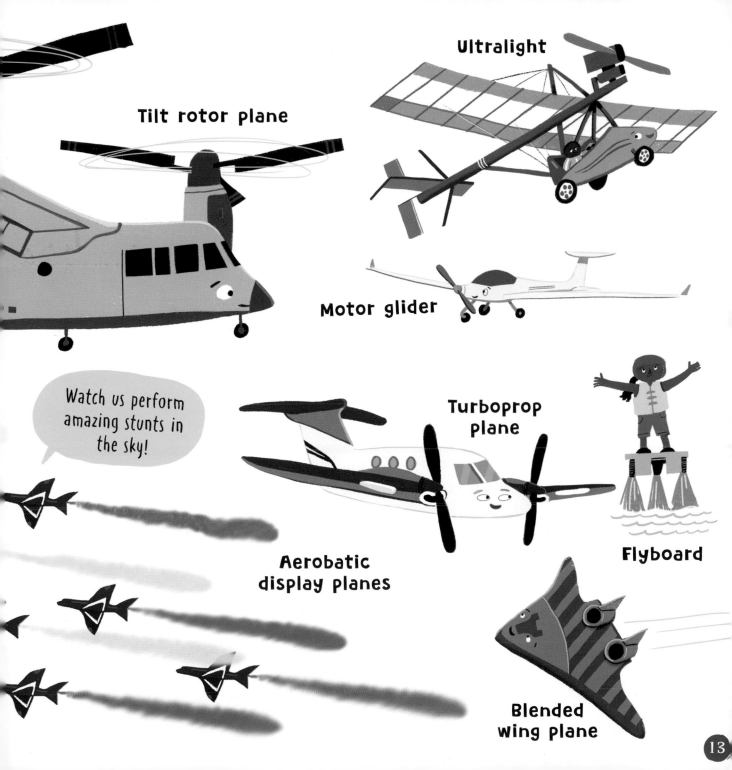

Ultralight

Tilt rotor plane

Motor glider

Watch us perform amazing stunts in the sky!

Turboprop plane

Aerobatic display planes

Flyboard

Blended wing plane

13

Future of flight!

Technology is helping to make planes quieter and kinder to the environment. New types of aircraft are being invented all the time.

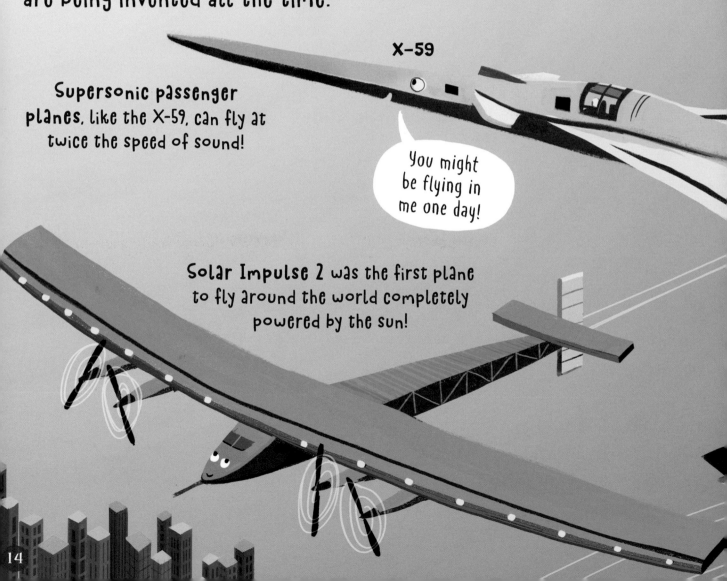

X-59

Supersonic passenger planes, like the X-59, can fly at twice the speed of sound!

You might be flying in me one day!

Solar Impulse 2 was the first plane to fly around the world completely powered by the sun!

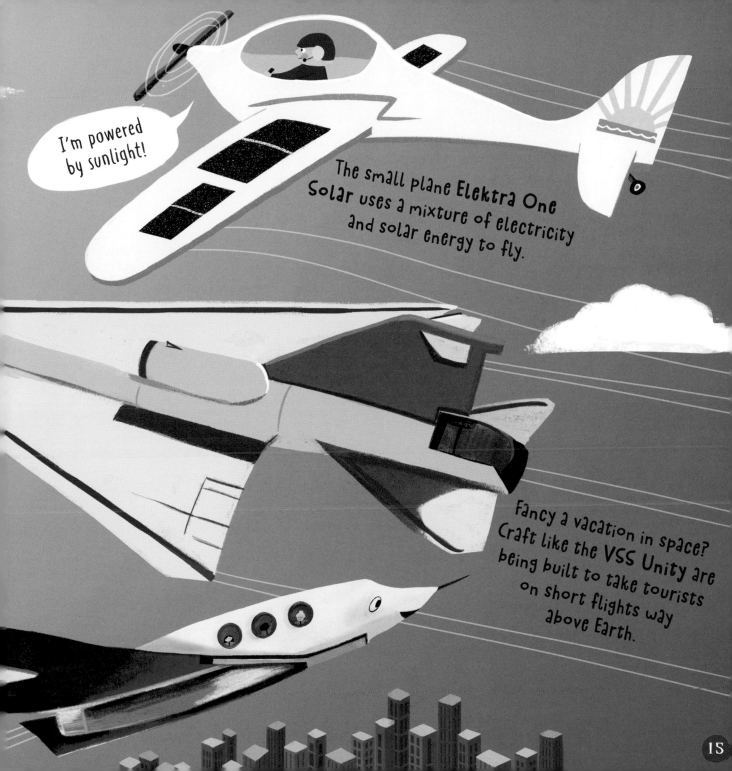

I'm powered by sunlight!

The small plane Elektra One Solar uses a mixture of electricity and solar energy to fly.

Fancy a vacation in space? Craft like the VSS Unity are being built to take tourists on short flights way above Earth.

15

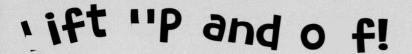 ift "P and o f!

Whomp! Whomp! Helicopters have spinning blades called rotors that lift them off the ground!

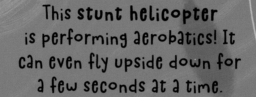

This **stunt helicopter** is performing aerobatics! It can even fly upside down for a few seconds at a time.

wooo!

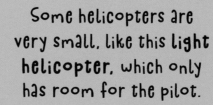

Some helicopters are very small, like this **light helicopter**, which only has room for the pilot.

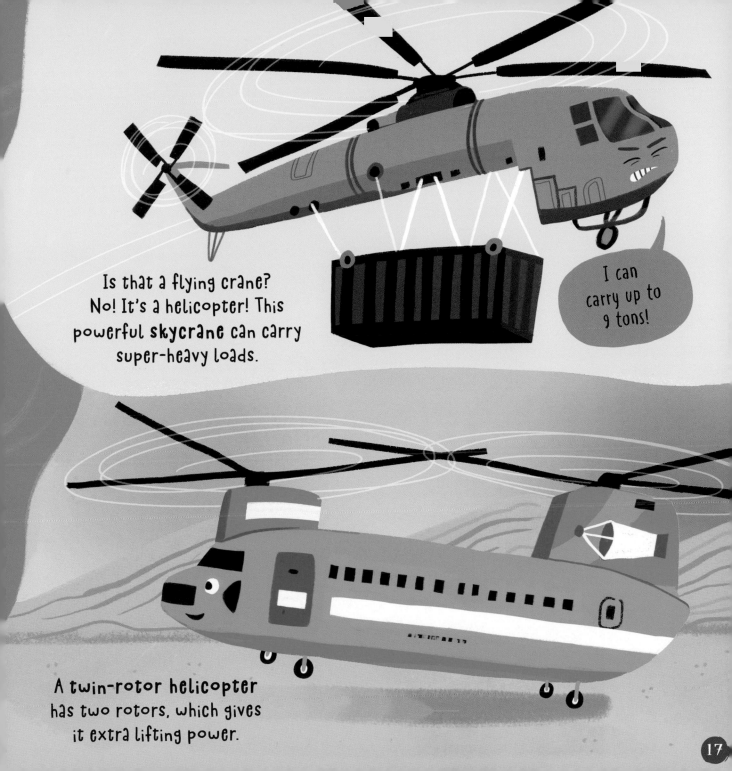

Is that a flying crane? No! It's a helicopter! This powerful **skycrane** can carry super-heavy loads.

I can carry up to 9 tons!

A twin-rotor helicopter has two rotors, which gives it extra lifting power.

Up and away!

Which aircraft can fly without an engine? A glider!

An engine-powered plane tows the glider up into the sky. Then it is released to glide and soar on the air!

Time to glide!

Tow line

What a view!

Control bar

Hang gliders set off from high places, such as hillsides, then the pilot glides to the ground using a control bar to steer.

19

Lighter than air

Hot-air balloons make use of the fact that warm air is lighter than cool air.

To take off, the pilot turns on the burner to heat up the air inside the hot-air balloon.

The first hot-air balloon took flight in 1783!

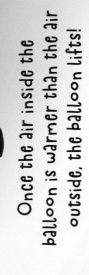

Once the air inside the balloon is warmer than the air outside, the balloon lifts!

To come back down, the pilot slowly lets air out of the balloon.

I make almost no noise!

The passengers stand with the pilot in the balloon's basket. This is also where the fuel is kept.

All about airships!

Sometimes called zeppelins or blimps, airships are filled with a gas called helium.

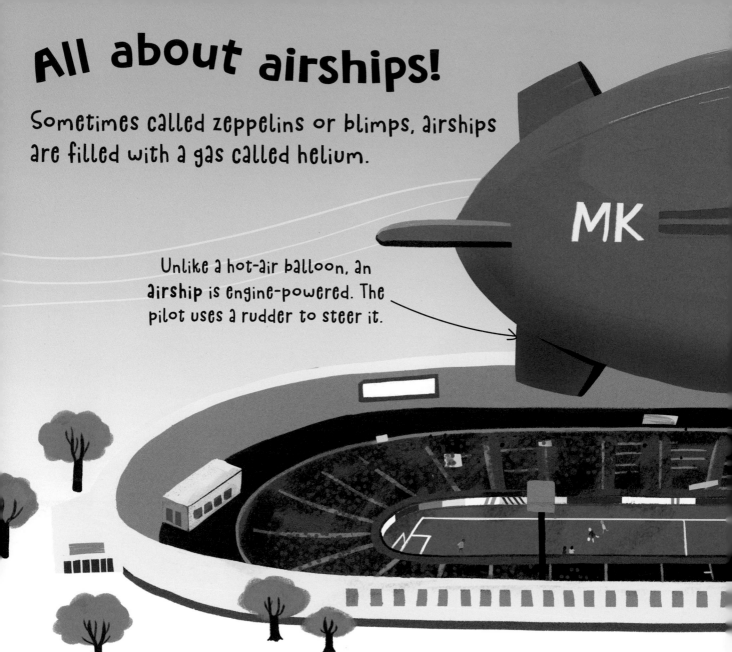

Unlike a hot-air balloon, an airship is engine-powered. The pilot uses a rudder to steer it.

To come down, the pilot pumps air, which is heavier than helium, into the main body of the airship – and slowly it sinks!

Nowadays, airships are used for advertising, research, and covering sporting events rather than carrying passengers.

MK

My propellers guide me backward or forward.

Under the airship is a cabin called a gondola. This is where the pilots and passengers sit.

Pilot

Controls

Drone Power!

Drones are a type of aircraft that can fly without a pilot.

A drone can be used for all kinds of things, from taking photos of Earth to delivering packages!

Knock, knock! Delivery!

Some drones are remote-controlled by someone on the ground, while others are programmed by a computer.